Strip
Patchwork

Lydia Fouché

δελος

CAPE TOWN

Also available in Afrikaans as *Bont Strooklas*

Translated by Hazel Petrig
Photography by Anton de Beer
Cover design by Abdul Amien
Book design by Debbie Odendaal
Typeset in 10 on 12 pt Optima by Martin Graphix, Cape Town
Printed and bound by Duncan Wulf Printing, Cape Town

First edition, first impression 1991

ISBN 1-86826-204-9

Contents

Introduction

I discovered the pleasures and design potential of patchwork quite by chance. Art and design are my main interests and the focus of my career, while needlework has been my favourite pastime since I was a child. Although I have always known about patchwork, it never really interested me. I did not have the time or the patience for traditional handwork methods, while conventional patterns and fabric designs had never really inspired me to tackle a patchwork project. I find the design process more satisfying than following all the rules to master a precise technique.

What finally persuaded me to investigate the design possibilities of various patchwork methods was a book on the work of the Amish in America, as well as photographs of wall hangings by world-famous textile artists. Suddenly I realised the wonderfully creative possibilities of this medium.

Although I have never taken formal courses in patchwork or any other techniques, I firmly believe that you need to know the rules before you can successfully deviate from them. So I try to read as many books on various patchwork techniques as possible and to view exhibitions of patchwork whenever I can.

The joining technique described in this book is just one of many which interest me. It is based on ordinary strip patchwork and Seminole work, two well-known methods about which much has been written. What appeals to me about these methods is that they enable one to try out many different variations, particularly regarding colour combinations, without being too time-consuming. The purpose of my book is therefore not to say something new about the technique, but rather to illustrate the diverse possibilities of colour usage.

I know so many people who believe creativity is something only the lucky few have been born with. I believe that most people possess a latent creativity, but that they seldom have enough self-confidence to take their ideas further. My book therefore aims to illustrate the exciting design possibilities of a simple technique, but one with interesting colour combinations, and to inspire readers to start experimenting with colour and design themselves.

General information

All the examples in this book are based on the principles of strip patchwork and Seminole work, which is why it's simply called "Strip Patchwork". With strip patchwork strips of fabric are sewn together and then cut in various ways to be joined again in new combinations. What makes this work so exciting is the infinite range of design opportunities. It's almost like turning a kaleidoscope – by merely changing a colour or turning a block, a completely new pattern is formed.

For the purposes of the book a few basic designs are discussed with reference to a range of cushion covers, because the simple cover illustrates the colour and pattern principles well. However, the designs can be used for anything from a bed quilt to items of clothing. In the last chapter instructions are given for making a few domestic items for everyday use in the home.

Last but not least, I believe that there are only two golden rules for all forms of needlework and handwork: accuracy and neatness. Those who think that because an article is handmade it need not be finished off very well, should examine the handwork of Western Europe: if anything it's neater and more perfect than the machine-made article!

Principles of colour usage

Most books on patchwork have comprehensive and sometimes complicated sections dealing with colour theory. Knowledge of the so-called colour rules is useful, but don't allow them to dampen your instinctive feel for colour.

If you have a good feel for colour, you will often unconsciously make the right colour choices. With a little experimentation you will also invent new and exciting colour combinations. If you don't have the self-confidence to deviate from the more common colour schemes, learn about colour usage by concentrating on your surroundings – you'll see wonderful examples of exotic and striking colour combinations! There are many sources of inspiration – from the world of nature (take a closer look at the variety of colours that often appear together on a single flower) to the colourful pattern of sun umbrellas on the beach.

Textile fabrics provide a rich source of colour inspiration – from Oriental carpets to upholstery fabrics. Note that the fabrics which always catch your eye usually break one of the colour rules by, for example, using red, magenta and purple together or putting all the primary colours together. The secret lies not in *which* colours you use together, but *how* you do so.

By examining well-designed textile fabrics closely, you will soon discover what makes unusual colour combinations successful. Usually strong contrasting and clashing colours are only used in small areas, and with due consideration for the balance and composition of the whole, but even then there is always someone who will successfully break this "rule"!

The best way of choosing colours for a specific design is to put together all the shades you have of the selected colours. Remove those which don't look right and leave the rest for a day or so in a place where you can look at them often. A colour which doesn't tone in will soon bother you. If you need to buy more fabric, take all the colour samples to the shop with you.

The choice of fabric

Any patchwork is time-consuming. It is therefore not worth using a poor quality fabric; you should work with the best fabric you can afford.

TYPES OF FABRIC
Preferably use pure cotton for strip patchwork, especially if you are a beginner. When you are more experienced, you will find ways of using more "difficult" fabrics successfully. I prefer working with pure cotton, and because I usually do my quilting on a sewing machine, I normally use a good quality poplin (sailcloth) or chintz. The patterns in this book concentrate mainly on the design possibilities of colour. It is advisable not to use different types of fabric in one article, because the different textures may make the design look overdone.

BATTING
All the strip patchwork items discussed here have a layer of batting for reinforcement, and any type of batting may be used.

COLOUR OF FABRIC
I have used plain coloured fabrics throughout for the designs in this book, because of the strong graphic effects which can be achieved with them. The total colour spectrum is often used in one design. Printed fabrics must be used with great caution in such designs, as they tend to look garish.

It is often difficult to get enough colours in the same type of fabric at one shop. This has made me a keen fabric "collector". Whenever I come across a new colour, I usually buy a metre and stash it away until I need it. If you do this you will quickly build up a wide range of colours.

PREPARATION OF FABRIC
It is important to pre-shrink all fabrics in warm water before use. By doing this you can tell immediately whether the fabric is colourfast or not. If the fabric colour runs, immerse the fabric for ten minutes in a mixture of 125 ml vinegar and 2 ℓ water, and then rinse it in clean water. If you are going to use the fabric for a wall hanging or a similar article which is seldom washed, it will not matter much if it is not entirely colourfast. Fabrics for clothing must always be 100% colourfast.

Another problem often encountered with inferior fabrics is that strong light causes them to fade after a while. Avoid using such fabrics if you would like your work to become an heirloom!

QUANTITY OF FABRIC REQUIRED FOR A PROJECT
The required amount of fabric is given in strip widths for all projects. This makes it easier to calculate the total amount of fabric required, because the strips are cut across the full width of the fabric. Count how many strips of a particular colour are used, multiply it by the width required and allow 10 cm for safety. Some shops only sell full or half metres of fabric, so keep any remnants for later projects.

Materials

The basic equipment for strip patchwork is a sewing machine, a good pair of scissors, ruler and pencil. Other equipment is available to make handwork easier and enable you to produce a much neater and more professionally finished article. The equipment mentioned below is readily available and should not cost a fortune. However, it does not pay to buy on the cheap, especially when it comes to items like a rotary cutter and a pair of scissors.

SEWING MACHINE

Any make of sewing machine with a neat and accurate straight stitch.

ROTARY CUTTER

This cutter is essential for the fast and accurate cutting of the long strips of fabric required for strip patchwork. The more expensive type of rotary cutter is by far the best, although the blades are very costly and must be handled with care. They are easily damaged when you accidently cut over a hard object like a pin, and can injure a careless person rather severely. Keep them away from children at all times.

CUTTING BOARD

A cutting board is essential if you use a rotary cutter, otherwise your work surface will be cut to shreds. Various types are available. Most needlework shops sell the nylon-type board in sizes of 1 m x 1 m and 1 m x 2 m, while handcraft shops sell a rubber mat with graph squares. The squares are a great help to ensure that the fabric and cutting line are at right angles.

STRIP RULERS

Some shops specialising in accessories for patchwork sell very useful Perspex rulers with lines indicating various widths. If you cannot find these rulers, make similar ones by having a sheet of Perspex cut into different widths. You may also use the commercial steel rulers, but be careful not to hit the ruler with the rotary cutter, because this will damage its blade rather badly.

90° TRIANGLE OR TRY SQUARE

This is used to ensure that the edge of the fabric is at a perfect right angle before cutting. Keep a protractor or adjustable set square at hand while you work, because angles other than 90° are also sometimes used.

SOFT PENCIL

Preferably use a B or HB pencil for marking.

PINS

Good, long, thin, rust-free pins are essential for accuracy.

IRON AND IRONING BOARD

A good, clean iron, preferably a steam iron, and a sturdy ironing surface should be conveniently situated near the sewing machine, as seams often have to be pressed.

General instructions

In all the designs discussed here, strips of fabric are joined to form a series of strips. The strips may be narrow or wide, so that one design may comprise a number of strips of varying widths. Colours can be chosen to flow softly from one colour in the colour spectrum to the next to encompass the whole spectrum, or they can be strongly contrasting.

The basic series of strips may be the end product, or it can be cut into block strips and then joined to form another pattern. This is why strip patchwork is so exciting, because you can obtain an almost infinite variety of designs in this way.

Methods and colour combinations are explained with reference to a range of cushion covers. The finishing of the cushion covers is described on p. 9.

Terms

STRIP
A strip of fabric cut according to the basic method.

STRIP SERIES
A variety of strips joined according to the basic method.

BLOCK STRIP
A strip cut from a strip series. It may also be cut at an angle to form a diamond pattern.

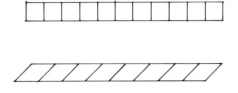

BLOCK STRIP SERIES
A series of block strips which have been joined together.

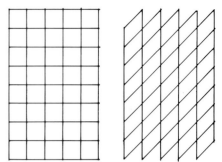

Basic methods

The following guidelines apply to all the articles described in the book, except where otherwise indicated in the instructions.

CUTTING OF STRIPS
Strips of fabric are always cut across the full width of the fabric. Fold the piece of fabric in half, right sides inwards, with the selvedges matching. Lay the fabric flat so that the folded selvedges lie horizontally at the bottom. Use a 90° triangle or a try square to check that the edge of the fabric where you will start cutting is at a right angle to the fold line. Trim the edge straight with a rotary cutter if necessary, otherwise the strips will not be straight when folded open. (The fabric may be folded again so that you can cut through four layers simultaneously.)

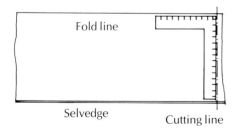

Use a rotary cutter and strip ruler to cut strips to the desired width. Retain the remnants if the full strips are not used, as they can be joined together later to form part of a new design.

JOINING OF STRIPS
All seams are stitched 7 mm wide, called a machine foot width. A machine foot width is the distance from the middle of the pressure foot of the sewing machine (the middle needle position) to the outer edge of the right prong. It is therefore very easy to ensure that the seams are the same width, as the edge of the strip will always be flush with the edge of the foot as you sew.

I cannot emphasise enough how important accuracy is when doing strip patchwork. If the seams are not the same width from the start, you will never get the corners of the blocks to align precisely at a later stage, and the finished product will always look slightly sloppy.

It is preferable to change the direction in which you stitch the strips together each time; if you don't do this the joined strips tend to pull slightly skew, which can hamper accuracy, especially with block patterns.

Note: Because all designs described in this book are finished off with a layer of batting, it is not necessary to zigzag or overlock seams.

CUTTING OF BLOCK STRIPS
When a series of strips has been joined and pressed, a block strip is cut as follows: Place the try square at a right angle on one corner of the strips, and cut the raw edge straight. Cut the block strips as wide as required, and check after every few strips that the cutting edge is still at a right angle to the strips.

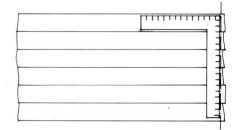

JOINING OF BLOCK STRIPS

Place block strips on top of each other in pairs, right sides facing, making sure that the seams between blocks are exactly on top of each other (except in designs where the blocks do not line up). Pin each spot where the seams align and stitch together with a 7 mm seam. Press the seams, all in the same direction.

PRESSING OF SEAMS

Press seams between strips so that they all lie in the same direction. This makes it much easier to join block strips later. Note: Do not press seams open, both parts of each seam must lie to the one side. It is very important to handle the patchwork carefully while pressing, because it can lose its shape when stretched too much. Make sure that the whole seam is pressed flat neatly, and does not pucker.

MACHINE-QUILTING THE FINISHED DESIGN

Each design is finished by laying the strip patchwork on a layer of batting and machine-quilting through both layers. Use a stitch length of 2 mm and sew along each long seam. Pull the seams open slightly while working so the stitching will not be noticeable.

The quilting can also be done at right angles to the striped designs as in stripe variation A – see photograph. Make fold lines equidistant from each other on the front and stitch along these lines. Because the stitches will show here, choose a thread which will match the colour scheme of the design.

Finishing of cushion covers

This is a quick and neat method of making cushion covers which can be easily removed for washing.

Depending on the size required for the finished cover, a border is usually added. The border puts the finishing touch to the object and can help to bring the various designs and colours together nicely. If black or navy blue are used as contrasting colours in a design, they are usually good colour choices for borders. The colour scheme of the area where the cushions will be placed should guide your choice of colour for the border.

Note: All the designs depicted in the photographs in the following chapter have borders, but the strips required are not listed among the materials. See below for these border strip requirements.

MATERIALS

- Completed design for the front of the cover
- Two or three (depending on the size of the cover) strips each 50 mm wide in the colour chosen for the border
- One strip in the colour chosen above, 35 mm wide x 25 long
- A piece of fabric in the colour chosen above for the back of the cover, as wide as the finished front, but 20 mm longer
- A piece of batting, the size of the finished front plus the border strips

METHOD

1 Cut from each of the 50 mm-wide strips a piece as long as one side of the front. Sew these strips to two opposite sides of the front and press the seams towards the outside. Cut pieces from the rest of the strips for the remaining two sides (plus border strips) and stitch together.

2 Cut the batting to the exact size of the finished front, place against the wrong side and tack together firmly according to diagram 1.

3 Machine-quilt through both layers along the main seams as described on p. 8.

4 Place the 25 cm-long strip on the front in the middle of one of the short border strips, right sides facing, and stitch them together. Cut the batting along the seam, fold the strip back, right side up, and press (diagram 2).

5 Place the front and the fabric for the back together with right sides facing and cut the back to the exact size of the front, inclusive of the joined strip (this forms a facing).

6 Stitch around the edge according to diagram 3.

7 Carefully trim the batting back along the seam, mitre the corners and turn the cover right side out. Fold the short strips and facing to the inside to form a neatly finished opening and press carefully. (Do not put too much pressure on the iron, as the batting tends to flatten.)

8 Insert a cushion in the cover and close the opening with invisible stitches.

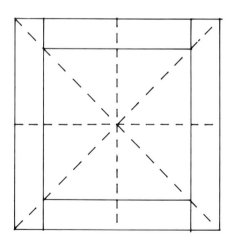

Diagram 1

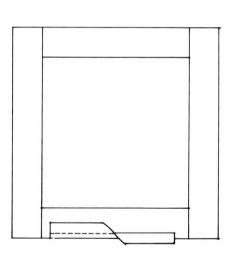

Diagram 2

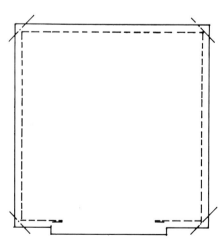

Diagram 3

Designs

Basic stripe designs

Most of the designs discussed here are based on the stripe design. The following variations illustrate what influence colour combinations and strip widths can have on the design.

STRIPE VARIATION A

MATERIALS

■ One strip 50 mm wide in each of the following colours:
1. Cream
2. Bright yellow
3. Orange
4. Red
5. Maroon
6. Purple
7. Dark blue
8. Bright blue
9. Sea-green
10. Bottle-green

METHOD

1 Assemble the strips in the order 1 to 10 – see photograph.

2 Stitch the strips together as described on p. 7.

3 Press the strips carefully with a steam iron so that the seams all lie in the same direction. Remember: Do not press the seams open.

4 Place a try square at right angles to the stripes on one edge of the strip series and cut the edge straight.

5 Measure the width of the strip series and cut off a square piece. Keep the remaining piece for further designs, e.g. block or diamond variations.

6 Finish the article as for a cushion cover (see method on p. 9) or keep it as a basis for further block designs.

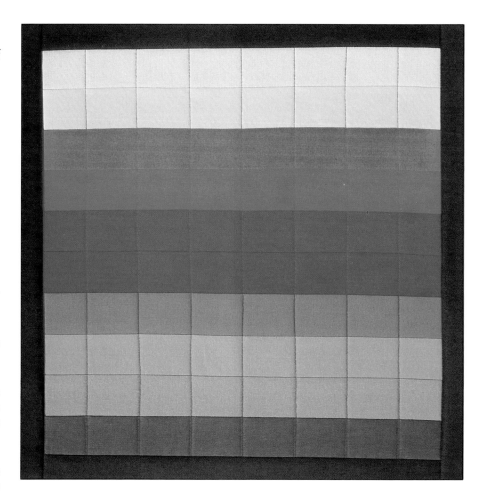

STRIPE VARIATION B

This design follows exactly the same method as for variation A, but only a few basic colours are used. The colours are arranged to flow harmoniously from one shade to the other.

MATERIALS

- One strip 50 mm wide in each of the following colours:
  1. Pale blue
  2. Bright blue
  3. Cobalt blue
  4. Purple
  5. Magenta
  6. Pale magenta
  7. Dark pink
  8. Bright pink
  9. Pale pink
  10. Pinky white

Note: Make sure that the three basic colours (pink, blue and purple) go together. It is also very important to ensure that the colours used are various shades of the same basic colour, for example the magentas and pinks, otherwise they will not tone in well.

METHOD

1 Arrange the strips in the order 1 to 10 – see photograph.

2 Follow the same methods as for stripe variation A.

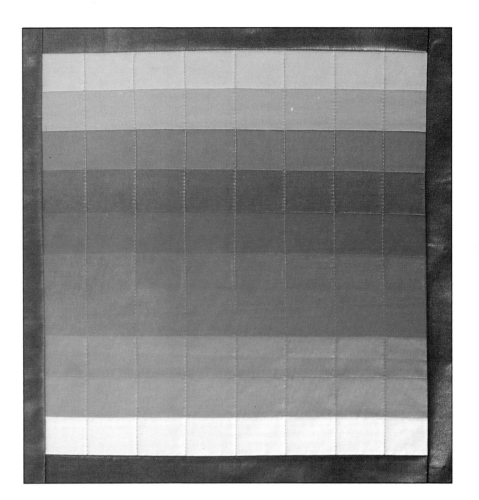

STRIPE VARIATION C

In this variation wide and narrow strips are alternated. The wide strips are from the same colour range as in stripe variation A (bright colours from the full colour spectrum), while the narrow strips are all black. The black lends the bright colours a glow, and the effect is similar to that of a stained-glass window.

MATERIALS

- Six strips each 35 mm wide in black
- One strip 50 mm wide in each of the following colours:
1. Bright yellow
2. Orange
3. Red
4. Maroon
5. Purple
6. Bright blue
7. Sea-green

METHOD

1 Arrange the strips in the order 1 to 7, alternating each colour strip with a narrow black strip – see photograph.

2 Follow the same methods as for stripe variation A.

Note: This design is also very effective when colours from the range used in stripe variation B are combined with dark dove grey.

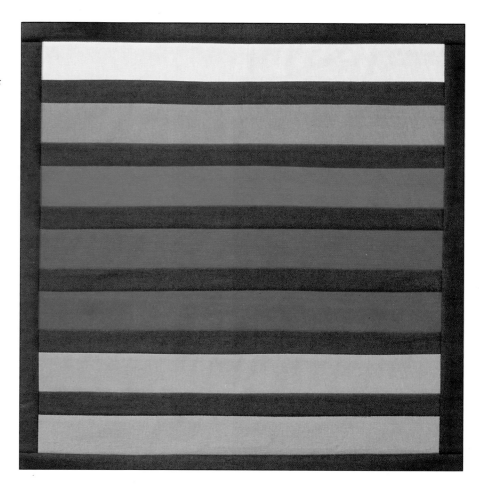

STRIPE VARIATION D

In this variation colours are contrasted with their complementary colours. Bright colours from the whole spectrum, and narrow and wide strips, are used.

MATERIALS

- One strip 50 mm wide in each of the following colours:
1. Bright yellow
2. Orange
3. Red
4. Maroon
5. Bright blue
6. Sea-green
7. Bottle-green
- One strip 35 mm wide in each of colours 1, 2, 3, 5, 6 and 7

METHOD

1 Stitch the strips together in the following order (the wide strips are indicated as W and the narrow strips as N): 1W, 7N, 2W, 6N, 3W, 5N, 4W, 3N, 5W, 2N, 6W, 1N, 7W – see photograph.

2 Follow the same method as for stripe variation A.

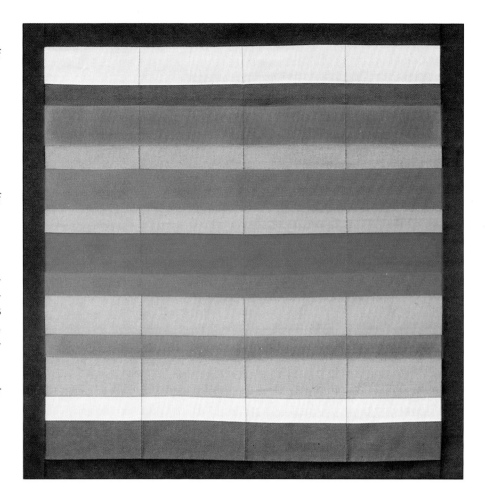

Block designs

For block designs a strip series is first required. This is cut into block strips and then joined together in a new pattern. All the block designs described here are based on the previous stripe designs.

One strip series, made of 120 cm strip lengths (the width of most fabrics), is enough for a cover comprising one stripe design and one block design. There will be a piece left over which can be used with other remnant strips in one of the mixed designs on pp. 23 and 24.

BLOCK VARIATION A

MATERIALS

One strip series made according to stripe variation A

METHOD

1 Make sure that one edge of the strip series is cut straight and at a right angle to the stripes.

2 Cut ten block strips each 50 mm wide from this strip series. (Remember to check that the edge of the fabric is still at a right angle to the stripes after every few cuts, otherwise it must be cut straight again.)

3 Assemble the block strips next to one another on the work surface, but turn every second strip so that the colours run in the opposite direction – see photograph.

4 Place the strips in pairs on top of each other, right sides facing. (A cream block at the top of a strip must be placed on a bottle-green block each time.)

5 Pin each pair of strips together carefully, making sure that all the seams are precisely aligned.

6 Stitch the pinned strips together as described on p. 8.

7 Without pressing the joined strips (too much handling can stretch the

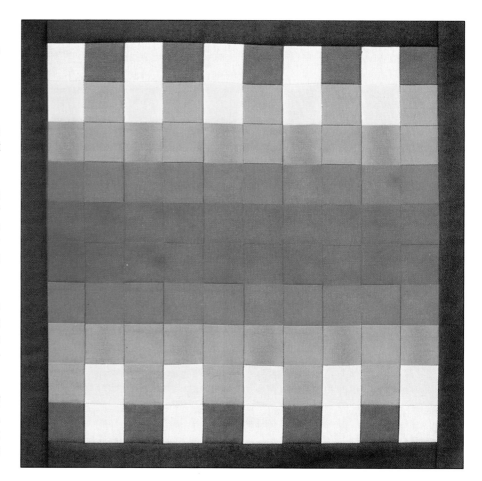

strips, making it difficult to match them precisely), assemble them in pairs again and repeat the stitching process until all ten strips have been joined.

8 Press the work carefully so that all seams lie to one side.

9 If you have worked accurately, the edges will be fairly straight. If not, cut them straight with a rotary cutter and ruler.

10 Finish the design as a cushion cover – see method on p. 9.

BLOCK VARIATION B

MATERIALS

- One strip series made according to stripe variation B
- One very pale grey-blue strip, 50 mm wide

METHOD

1 Make sure that one edge of the strip series is cut straight and at a right angle to the stripes.

2 Cut five block strips each 50 mm wide from the strip series.

3 Take the remaining piece of the strip series and stitch the grey-blue strip to the light blue side. Unpick the last pale pink strip on the other side and press the seam again.

4 Cut five block strips each 50 mm wide from this new strip series.

5 Lay the first and second groups of block strips alternately next to each other, with the pink and pinky white blocks on top – see photograph.

6 Place the strips in pairs on top of each other, right sides facing. Pin every second strip carefully, making sure that all the seams are precisely aligned, and stitch together.

7 Without pressing the seams of the joined strips, place them in pairs again and repeat the stitching process until all the strips have been joined.

8 Press the work carefully so that all the seams lie in the same direction.

9 If you have worked accurately, the edges will be flush. If not, cut them straight with a rotary cutter and ruler.

10 Finish the design as for a cushion cover – see method on p. 9.

BLOCK VARIATION C

MATERIALS

- One strip series made according to stripe variation C
- Six black strips, each 35 mm wide

METHOD

1 Make sure that one edge of the strip series is at a right angle to the stripes and then cut off seven block strips, each 50 mm wide.

2 Pin a narrow black strip to a block strip and stitch together. Repeat until six of the block strips have been joined to black strips in this way.

3 Press the strips very lightly with the seams lying towards the black strips, and cut the black strips to align with the block strips. Place the joined strips in pairs on top of each other, right sides facing, with all the yellow blocks at the top – see photograph. Pin the strips together carefully, making sure that the colours are in the correct order. Stitch the strips together in pairs.

4 Repeat until all the strips have been joined. Then stitch the remaining block strip to the last black strip.

5 Press the seams towards the vertical black strips so that they face each other in pairs on every black strip.

6 Cut the edges straight and finish as for a cushion cover – see method on p. 9.

BLOCK VARIATION D

MATERIALS

One strip series made according to stripe variation D

METHOD

1 Making sure that one edge of the strip series is straight and at a right angle to the stripes, cut off nine block strips each 50 mm wide.

2 Assemble the strips alongside one another, with all the yellow blocks at the top. Move the strip second from left half a block up, so that the bottom edge of the narrow bottle-green block is right opposite the top edge of the narrow bottle-green block of the left strip – see photograph. Also shift strips 4, 6 and 8 up half a block.

3 Place the strips in pairs on top of one another, right sides facing, and pin together carefully. Check that the corresponding seams lie exactly on top of one another.

4 Stitch the strips together in pairs.

5 Without pressing the seams, pin the joined strips together again in pairs and stitch. Repeat until all the strips have been joined.

6 Press all the seams carefully to one side.

7 Cut the edges straight and finish as for a cushion cover – see method on p. 9.

Diamond designs

The diamond designs are very similar to block designs, except the block strips are cut at an angle to form a diamond pattern. The block strip consists of a series of small diamonds instead of a series of small blocks.

DIAMOND VARIATION A

MATERIALS

- One strip series made according to stripe variation A
- Large protractor or adjustable set square
- Soft pencil

METHOD

1 Using the set square as a base, draw a line at an angle of 45 degrees from the top cream-coloured strip to the bottom bottle-green strip.

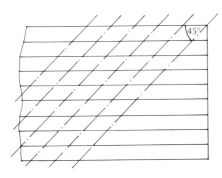

2 Cut along this line with a rotary cutter and ruler. Keep the remnant, as it can be used in one of the mixed variations described on p. 23.

3 Cut ten strips each 50 mm wide at this angle.

4 Lay the strips on top of each other in pairs, right sides facing, with the cream blocks on top of the bottle-green blocks. Make sure that the seams between blocks are in line when the two strips are folded open. Pin together.

Note: It is more difficult to line up these seams than in the case of block patterns, because all the cross-seams are now at an angle. If you have prepared the strip series very accurately and pressed them very carefully, the seams should correspond precisely.

5 Stitch the strips together in pairs.

6 Without first pressing the seams, repeat the process until all the strips have been joined – see photograph.

7 Press all the seams carefully to one side.

8 Using the try square, cut the two serrated sides straight and at right angles to the other sides.

9 Finish as for a cushion cover – see method on p. 9.

DIAMOND VARIATION B

MATERIALS

- One strip series made according to stripe variation B
- Protractor or adjustable set square
- Soft pencil

METHOD

1 Using the set square as a base, draw a line at an angle of 80 degrees from the top pinky white strip to the bottom pale blue strip. Cut along this line with a rotary cutter and ruler.

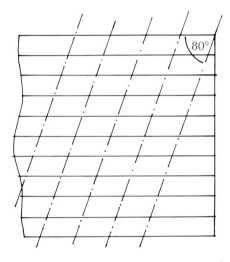

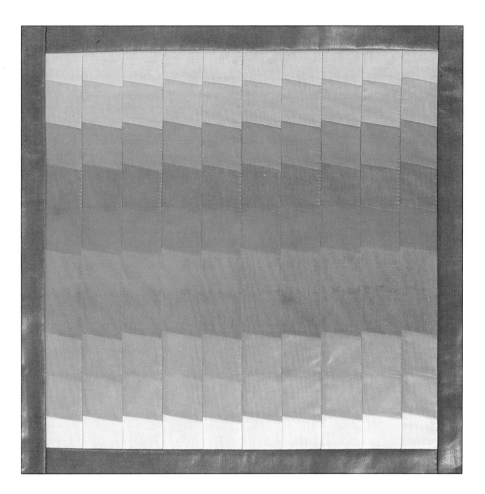

2 Cut ten strips each 50 mm wide at this angle.

3 From this point on follow the same method as for diamond variation A. You will notice however that the seams between the small diamonds are not aligned in this case.

DIAMOND VARIATION C

In this variation the whole pattern does not consist of small diamonds, as for the previous two variations. A few diamond strips are alternated with black strips.

MATERIALS

- One strip series made according to stripe variation D
- Two black strips, each 35 mm wide, cut through in the middle to make four strips
- Soft pencil

METHOD

1 Make sure that one edge of the strip series is flush and then cut off a square piece with sides as long as the width of the strip series.

2 Make a pencil mark on the top edge of the piece exactly 50 mm from the right-hand corner and then another three marks, each 50 mm apart. Mark the bottom edge precisely 50 mm from the left-hand corner and then make another three marks 50 mm apart. Connect the top and bottom marks with a pencil line.

3 Cut along these lines with a rotary cutter and ruler. Leave the strips and pieces on either side in the precise position in which they were cut. (As a further variation the central strip can be turned around so that the colours run in the opposite direction.)

4 Pin the black strips to the pieces on either side and to the diamond strips according to the photograph. Pin and stitch together in pairs and then do the same again with the joined pieces. Handle the strips very carefully, as they are cut on the bias and can stretch easily. If the strip series has been accurately prepared and the block strips carefully handled, the stripes should line up nicely.

5 Press the seams carefully towards the black strips.

6 Cut the edges straight and finish as for a cushion cover – see method on p. 9.

Windmills

This section deals with the effects which can be obtained by cutting strip series into triangles and then joining them to form squares. New colour combinations are also used.

WINDMILL VARIATION A

MATERIALS

■ Seven navy blue strips, each 35 mm wide
■ One strip 50 mm wide, in each of the following colours:
1. Scarlet
2. Dark red
3. Maroon
4. Bright blue
5. Light blue

METHOD

1 Make a strip series according to the basic method by alternating the strips in the order 1 to 5 with strips of navy blue, but only using four strips of navy blue.

2 Make sure that one edge of the strip series is straight and at a right angle to the strips. Cut two squares from it and cut each square into two triangles.

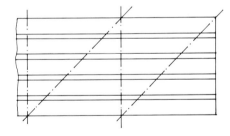

3 Stitch the triangles together in pairs with a navy blue strip in the middle – see photograph for colour sequence.

4 Press the seams carefully so that they lie towards the navy blue strips.

5 Stitch the long sides of the two joined triangles to either side of a navy blue strip. Press the seams, again towards the navy blue strip.

6 Straighten the sides of the finished square with the rotary cutter.

7 Stitch a navy blue strip to each of the two opposite sides of the joined square, press the seams to the outside and do the same with the other two sides.

8 Finish as for a cushion cover – see method on p. 9.

21

WINDMILL VARIATION B

MATERIALS

One strip 50 mm wide, in each of the following colours:
1. Pale blue
2. Bright blue
3. Purple
4. Magenta
5. Pink

METHOD

1 Make a strip series according to the basic method by stitching the strips together in the order 1 to 5.

2 Make sure that one edge of the strip series is straight and at a right angle to the stripes and cut four squares from it.

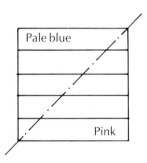

3 Place the squares on top of each other in pairs, right sides facing, with a pale blue strip on top of a pink strip.

4 Make a diagonal cut across each square to form two triangles.

5 Keeping the triangles in the exact position in which they were cut, pin each set of two pieces lying on top of one another together along the diagonal. Stitch together.

6 Press the seams of the joined squares carefully towards the side where the triangles are predominantly blue. Make sure that you do not distort the squares in the process.

7 Pin and stitch together the joined squares in pairs – see photograph for colour sequence. Press the seams.

8 Stitch the two joined rectangles together – see photograph for colour sequence. Press the seams.

9 Finish as for a cushion cover – see method on p. 9.

Combining variations

This section illustrates how you can combine the variations that have been shown previously. By doing this, you can also use up most of the remnants.

MIXED VARIATION A

MATERIALS

■ One strip series made according to stripe variation D (The remnants of diamond variations A and B can also be used for similar designs, but adjustments will have to be made because the finished article must be square.)
■ One maroon strip, 50 mm wide (cut in two)
■ One bright blue strip (cut in two) and one sea-green strip (half the length of a bright blue strip), each 35 mm wide

METHOD

1 Making sure that one edge of the strip series is straight and at a right angle to the stripes, cut a piece 21 cm wide from it.

2 Make a pencil mark on the top edge exactly 50 mm from the right-hand corner, and another mark 50 mm from the left-hand corner on the bottom edge. Join the marks with a pencil line and then cut along this line to form two triangles.

3 Make a strip series with the remaining strips by joining them in the following order: bright blue, maroon, sea-green, maroon, bright blue.

4 Pin the strip series to the diagonal side of one of the triangles and stitch together. Cut the edges straight. Stitch the other triangle to the other side of the strip series to form a square – see photograph. Cut the edges straight.

5 Finish as for a cushion cover – see method on p. 9.

23

MIXED VARIATION B

This variation combines the block design and the windmill design.

MATERIALS

- Six black strips, each 25 mm wide
- Three black strips, each 35 mm wide, for border
- One purple strip, 25 mm wide, cut into 7 equal pieces
- One strip 161 mm wide, and one strip 25 mm wide, in each of the following colours:
1. Magenta
2. Bright blue
3. Sea-green

METHOD

1 Make a strip series according to the basic method by alternating each of the wide strips in colours 1, 2 and 3 with a black strip of 25 mm wide. Start and end with coloured strips.

2 Making sure that one edge of the strip series is straight and at a right angle to the stripes, cut off two squares. Cut each square into two triangles as for windmill variation A.

3 Make another strip series by alternating each of the narrow strips in colours 1, 2 and 3 with a black strip of 25 mm wide. Start and end with a black strip.

4 Cut this strip series into six equal pieces and join them again with a purple strip between every two black strips. Start and end with a purple strip. Press the seams so they all lie to one side.

5 Making sure that one edge of this strip series is straight and at a right angle to the stripes, cut off two block strips 25 mm wide.

6 Take one of these block strips and carefully unpick the seams between the middle purple block and its adjoining black blocks. See photograph for colour sequence: pin and stitch together the triangles in pairs with half a block strip in between. Each time align the purple blocks with a black strip in the triangles.

7 Press the seams towards either side.

8 Pin and stitch together the joined triangles with the remaining block strip in between. A purple block must fall precisely in the middle and align with every black strip in the triangles – see photograph. Press the seams towards either side.

9 Join a black strip of 35 mm wide to two sides of the completed square, press towards the outside and repeat for the other two sides.

10 Finish as for a cushion cover – see method on p. 9.

Projects

Strip patchwork can be used for a wide variety of articles, especially wall hangings and bed quilts, because the method is so much faster than that of traditional patchwork. All too often someone has started a bed quilt for her child's room, only to complete it for her grandchild's! A few other articles which can be made by strip patchwork methods are clothing (for example, jackets), carry bags, tea-cosies and tray cloths. The following patterns will enable you to make unusual and useful items for yourself or as gifts for your friends.

Wall picture with fan pattern

MATERIALS

- One black strip, 50 mm wide, cut in two
- One black strip, 125 mm wide, cut in two
- Two magenta strips, each 35 mm wide
- One strip 50 mm wide x 50 cm long in each of the following colours:
1. Magenta
2. Maroon
3. Purple
4. Dark bottle-green
5. Sea-green
6. Turquoise
- Three black strips, each 8 cm wide, for border
- Big protractor or adjustable set square
- Soft pencil

METHOD (see cover photograph)

1 Make a strip series according to the basic method by joining the strips in the order 1 to 6.

2 Stitch one half of the 125 mm-wide black strip to the magenta strip and the other half to the turquoise strip.

3 With the magenta strip on top, make sure that the left edge of the strip series is flush. Make a pencil mark 20 mm from the top left-hand corner. With the aid of a protractor, draw a line at an angle of 80 degrees from top left to bottom right. Cut along this line.

4 Keep the cut-off section to one side and at the same angle cut seven block strips, each 35 mm wide, from the strip series. Cut another piece the same size as the cut-off piece from the rest of the strip series, but with the widest section (magenta) at the top right – see photograph.

5 Arrange the side pieces and block strips in a fan-shaped pattern according to the photograph. Move the first strip 20 mm higher than the left-hand side piece, the second strip 18 mm higher than the first strip and so on according to these measurements: 16 mm, 12 mm, 10 mm, 6 mm and 4 mm. Shift the right-hand side piece 2 mm higher than the last block strip. Stitch the strips together, following this pattern precisely.

6 Press the seams so that they all lie in the same direction.

7 With the aid of the try square, cut the black edges straight and at right angles to the other sides.

8 Stitch a 50 mm-wide black strip to each long side of the completed design and press the seams so that they face outwards.

9 Stitch a magenta strip to the top and bottom sides of the completed design, press the seams to the outside and stitch the rest of the strips to the remaining two sides. Press the seams.

10 Border: Stitch and press the 8 cm-wide black strip to the finished design as instructed above. This completes the front of the wall picture.

11 Finish off the wall picture as described for a cushion cover on p. 9, but do not sew on a short strip for the opening on one side; rather close the opening with invisible stitches. Frame the picture.

Wall hanging in pink and blue

MATERIALS

■ Two strips of 80 mm wide (W) and two strips of 35 mm wide (N) in each of the following colours, except where otherwise indicated (use fabric at least 120 cm wide):

1. Blue-white (2 x W and 1 x N)
2. Very pale blue
3. Pale blue
4. Bright blue
5. Blue-purple
6. Purple
7. Magenta-purple
8. Magenta (1 x W and 2 x N)

■ One strip in pale grey, 35 mm x 30 cm long
■ One strip in pale grey, 14 cm wide
■ 1,2 m pale grey fabric for back, 120 cm wide
■ 1,2 m batting, 120 cm wide
■ Dark grey strips for border, four 12 cm wide and two 16 cm wide

METHOD

1 Make two strip series according to the basic method. Arrange the first series as follows: N1, N2, W1, N3, W2, N4, W3, N5, W4, N6, W5, N7, W6, N8, W7. Also arrange strip series 2 in this way, starting at N2 and joining W8 to W7.

2 Press the seams of the two series of strips towards the paler strips.

3 Join strip series 1 to strip series 2 by stitching W8 to W7. Press the seam towards W7.

4 Make sure that the top and bottom edges of the joined piece are straight and at right angles to the stripes. Fold the piece in the middle by bringing the top and bottom edges together and then fold again in the middle. (The folds lie in the same direction as the stripes.)

5 Fold the folded piece in half width-wise. The fold will now lie at a right angle to the stripes.

6 Cut off block strips of the following widths from the folded strip series:
One strip 200 mm wide
Two strips each 125 mm wide
Two strips each 100 mm wide
Two strips each 75 mm wide
Eight strips each 50 mm wide

7 Assemble the strips alongside one another in the following order: 50 mm, 75 mm, 50 mm, 100 mm, 50 mm, 125 mm, 50 mm, 200 mm, 50 mm, 125 mm, 50 mm, 100 mm, 50 mm, 75 mm, 50 mm. Turn the block strip on both sides of the middle strip around so that a blue-white block lies on each side of the wide very pale blue block. Turn every second row to either side in this way – see photograph.

8 Pin the block strips together in pairs as they lie in front of you. Stitch together and repeat until all the block strips have been joined. Make sure you keep to the right sequence.

9 Press the seams carefully from the middle to either side.

10 Border: Join the 12 cm-wide dark grey strips in pairs across the width to form two long strips. Place these strips on each long side of the completed block strip series, making sure that the seams are precisely in the middle of the sides, and stitch together. Press the seams. Stitch the 16 cm-wide dark grey strips to the top and bottom of the strip series and press the seams. The front of the wall hanging is now complete.

11 Place the batting on the wrong side of the front and tack firmly.

12 Stitch the 30 cm-long pale grey strip to one of the short sides as described for the cushion cover on p. 9.

13 Cut the back exactly the same size as the front, tack all around the edge and finish off as for the cushion cover on p. 9.

14 Turn the wall hanging right side out and close the opening with invisible stitches. Press lightly.

15 Tack the front and back together well and machine-quilt all along the seams between the block strips. (A special quilting foot will make this easier.) Tie the loose threads together in pairs and work them in with a needle.

16 Make a casing through which a dowel or rod can be inserted for hanging up the finished article: hem the short sides of the 14 cm-wide pale grey strip, then turn up and iron in a hem of 2 cm along the long sides. Handstitch the casing to the back of the wall hanging, 2 cm from the top edge.

Bright tea-cosy and tray cloth

TEA-COSY

MATERIALS

- Two pale grey strips, each 50 mm wide
- Three pale grey strips, each 35 mm wide
- Seven bright yellow strips, each 50 mm wide
- Two bright yellow strips, each 35 mm wide
- 0,5 m unbleached calico for lining, 120 cm wide
- 0,5 m batting, 120 cm wide

METHOD

1 Make a strip series using three strips of each colour according to the basic method, alternating a wide yellow strip with a narrow grey strip.

2 Cut eight block strips each 35 mm wide from the strip series.

3 Cut ten pieces the same length as the above-mentioned block strips from the 50 mm-wide yellow strips.

4 Make two block strip series by alternating these block strips with the yellow strips. Use five yellow strips for every series and start and end with a yellow strip.

5 Measure one block strip series and then cut off two pieces of the same length from the first strip series.

6 Join the two block strip series and the two strip series together as follows: strip series, block strip series, strip series, block strip series.

7 Cut the batting and lining exactly the same size as the completed patchwork. Tack the patchwork onto the batting and then pin the patchwork

and lining together with right sides facing. Stitch along one long side.

8 Fold back the lining, lightly press the seam towards the lining and understitch the lining 2 mm from the seam according to the diagram.

9 Fold the lining back again and tack firmly through all layers. Machine-quilt along the length of the patchwork on the right side seam of every narrow strip.

10 Mark the middle of each of the four blocks on the unfinished long side. Fold the quilted patchwork double with the short sides facing and the right side facing inwards. Stitch the short sides together.

11 With the front still facing inwards, pull the four marks together – see top of tea-cosy in photograph. Pin and tack together the four seams thus formed. Stitch carefully so that all the seams join at the same spot and end each row of stitches with a few back-stitches.

12 Finish off all the seams and turn the completed tea-cosy right side out.

TRAY CLOTH

METHOD

1 Take the remaining piece of the strip series and join a 50 mm-wide yellow strip to the narrow grey strip. Cut off five block strips each 35 mm wide from this.

2 Alternately stitch the 50 mm-wide yellow strips and block strips together, starting and ending with a yellow strip. Press and cut the edges straight.

3 Border: Join wide grey strips to the long sides of this block strip series, press the seams towards the grey strips and repeat for the short sides. Repeat the process with the narrow yellow strips. This completes the front of the tray cloth.

4 Quilt and finish the cloth as described for the place mats on p. 32.

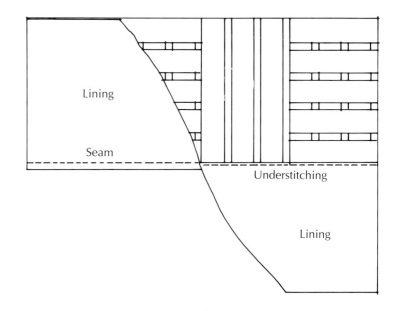

Rainbow quilt for a child's room

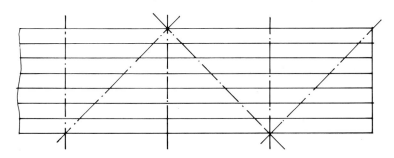

MATERIALS

- Four dark blue strips, each 266 mm wide
- Eleven dark blue strips, each 35 mm wide
- Four strips, each 50 mm wide, in each of the following colours:
1. Bright yellow
2. Orange
3. Red
4. Purple
5. Bright blue
6. Sea-green
7. Lime-green
- 2 m batting, 150 cm wide
- 2 m lining, 150 cm wide
- Dark blue strips for border: three 22 cm wide and four 12 cm wide

METHOD

1 According to the basic method, make the following strip series:
Series 1: Bright yellow, orange, red, purple, bright blue, sea-green, lime-green.
Series 2: Red, purple, bright blue, sea-green, lime-green, bright yellow, orange.
Series 3: Bright blue, sea-green, lime-green, bright yellow, orange, red, purple.
Series 4: Sea-green, lime-green, bright yellow, orange, red, purple, bright blue.

2 Ensuring that all the edges are at right angles to the stripes, place each strip series onto a 266 mm-wide dark blue strip, right sides facing. (If you have worked accurately, the strips and strip series should be equally wide. If not, cut them to the same width.)

3 Cut three squares from each strip series plus blue strip, and cut them into triangles according to the above diagram. Vary the directions in two of the series so that there are ultimately an equal number of triangles in both directions.

4 Keeping the pairs of triangles as they have been cut (a striped triangle should be lying precisely on a blue triangle every time), pin all the triangles together along their diagonals. Stitch together. Lightly press the seams so that they point towards the blue triangles.

5 Arrange the completed blocks on a flat surface and experiment with the various patterns which can be obtained by turning the blocks. The variations are endless! The diagrams illustrate two possibilities, while the example in the photograph is arranged completely differently.

6 Join the blocks as they are, or by using narrow dark blue strips. First join a row of blocks together and then join the rows. In the example in the photograph 35 mm-wide strips of the remaining pieces of the strip series were cut off and used together with dark blue strips to join the blocks.

7 Border: Stitch a 12 cm-wide dark blue strip to each long side (joining the strips if necessary). Press towards the blue strip. Stitch the 22 cm-wide dark blue strips to the short sides and press again. This completes the front of the quilt.

8 Attach the batting to the patchwork by machine-quilting all along the blocks.

9 Finish off the quilt as described for the wall hanging on p. 26, but without a casing for hanging.

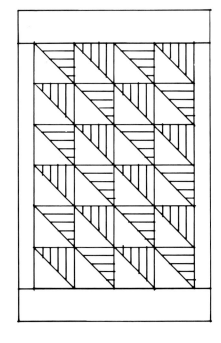

Place mats in blue and red

The pattern is for a set of four mats.

MATERIALS

- The following strips in both red and navy blue:
Two strips each 60 mm wide
Two strips each 45 mm wide
Two strips each 30 mm wide
- Six navy blue strips, each 55 mm wide
- Four bright blue strips, each 35 mm wide
- Four pieces of navy blue fabric, each 30 cm x 40 cm for the backs
- Four pieces of batting, each 30 cm x 40 cm

METHOD

1 Make two strip series according to the basic method, arranging the strips in this order: navy blue – 30 mm, red – 45 mm, navy blue – 60 mm, red – 60 mm, navy blue – 45 mm, red – 30 mm. Press the seams.

2 Make sure that one edge of each strip series is at a right angle to the stripes and cut off block strips of the following widths:
Eight strips each 30 mm wide
Eight strips each 45 mm wide
Eight strips each 60 mm wide
Four strips each 130 mm wide

3 Make four block strip series: arrange the block strips in such a way that a red block is always next to a navy blue block (see photograph) with strip widths from left to right 30 mm, 45 mm, 60 mm, 130 mm, 60 mm, 45 mm, 30 mm.

4 Press the seams of each series to

either side and cut the edges straight.

5 Border: Stitch a 35 mm-wide bright blue strip to each short side of the mats and press the seams towards the outside. Repeat the process for the long sides of the mats. Stitch 55 mm-wide navy blue strips to the short and long sides of the mats in the same way and press the seams. This completes the front of the mats.

6 Place a piece of batting on the wrong side of each front and tack firmly.

7 Place a back against each front, tack all along the edges and stitch

together, leaving an opening on one short side for turning inside out.

8 Carefully trim back the batting along the seams and mitre the corners.

9 Turn the mats right side out and close the openings with invisible stitches. Press lightly.

10 Tack the fronts and backs together firmly and machine-quilt all along the seams between the block strips. (A special quilting foot makes this easier.) Tie the loose threads together in pairs and work them in with a needle.